Weird Weather

Haydn Middleton

RIGBY

Contents

Introduction

Weather happens all over the world. Rain falls,
lightning strikes and wind blows somewhere on Earth
every day. Most of the time, the weather doesn't seem
very important to us. But sometimes, the weather gets
weird and strange things start to happen...

Stormy Weather

The Day it Rained Small Frogs

TROWBRIDGE, ENGLAND   17 JUNE, 1939

The sky went dark. It started to rain. The raindrops looked strange. They felt strange too. They were not drops of rain at all. Hundreds of small frogs were falling from the sky!

THAT'S WEIRD!   A strong wind once picked up crabs

What had happened?

The frogs had been picked up from a river! Storms can bring strong winds. Some strong winds spin round and round in circles. They suck things up from the ground and blow them around in the sky. Later, the things fall to the ground again, far from where the winds picked them up.

from the sea and dropped them in Worcester.

The Worst Wind in the World

GALVESTON, TEXAS, USA   8 SEPTEMBER, 1900

The winds blew so hard and so fast that they stirred up the sea. A huge wave smashed through Galveston. It wrecked buildings and thousands of people were hurt or killed.

THAT'S WEIRD!   A strong wind once made the blades

What had happened?

Galveston had been hit by a **hurricane**! Hurricanes are storms with strong winds and heavy rain. The winds start over warm seas. Then they turn into a storm with rain. The storms can grow up to 100 miles wide. Sometimes, hurricanes can be photographed from space.

of a windmill spin so fast that they caught on fire!

Sky Lights

Strike Out!

ATHLONE, IRELAND   27 OCTOBER, 1697

People heard a great clap of thunder. Then a flash lit up the sky. A zig-zag of light struck the castle and it began to burn. Then the castle blew up! The explosion smashed 64 houses!

THAT'S WEIRD! Lightning strikes somewhere on Earth

What had happened?

Lightning had struck the castle. Lightning is a huge spark in the sky. It strikes in stormy weather. Lightning can strike tall buildings again and again. People say that lightning never strikes the same place twice. That is not true!

bout 100 times every second.

The City in the Sky

ASHLAND, OHIO, USA
6 MARCH, 1890

In the city, the weather was calm. At first, the sky looked clear. Then people looked again. They saw a shape above them. The shape looked like a city in the sky!

THAT'S WEIRD! The top **horizon** in the photo above i≣

What had happened?

The city was a **mirage**! On calm days, warm air sits on top of cold air. The warm air and cold air make a mirror in the sky. That day, the mirror was **reflecting** a city.

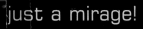

just a mirage!

Dark Days

The Big Blast

KRAKATAU ISLAND, INDONESIA
27 AUGUST, 1883

A big blast shook the earth. Dust from the blast blocked the light from the sun and the sky turned black. More than 36,000 people died in the blast and many more people were hurt.

THAT'S WEIRD!   After a volcano erupted in 1815, it

What had happened?

A **volcano** had erupted! When a volcano erupts, dust from the blast can block light from the sun. The blast from a volcano can cause important changes in weather too. The dust can keep the sun from warming the Earth. Then the weather turns cold.

snowed in summer!

Pea Soup City

LONDON, ENGLAND   5 DECEMBER, 1952

A thick cloud filled the air. The cloud was green and yellow. It looked like pea soup! The cloud was so thick that some people could not even see their feet. They walked into the River Thames by mistake!

THAT'S WEIRD! There are more houses in London toda

What had happened?

A cloud of **fog** had covered the city. Then smoke from the coal fires in people's homes got mixed with the fog. Smoke and fog together made "**smog**". For four days, there was no wind to blow the smog away. It just kept getting thicker and thicker.

than 50 years ago, but there is a lot less smog.

Walk on Water

LONDON, ENGLAND   WINTER, 1684

It was a very cold winter. It stayed cold for weeks and weeks. People were able to walk on the River Thames. They even built shops and theatres on the river!

What had happened?

The river had frozen! When water gets very cold, it freezes into ice. That winter, some people had fun with the ice and snow. But many people died from the cold too.

floated to Scotland on a lump of ice!

The Night of the Ice Rocks

MUNICH, GERMANY   12 JULY, 1984

It was a warm summer. But one day, a storm started. Lumps of ice rained down from the sky. They hit the ground like rocks. They smashed roofs and killed crops. The lumps of ice hurt 400 people!

THAT'S WEIRD!   In 1697, hailstones more than 60

What had happened?

The lumps of ice were **hailstones**. Hailstones are frozen raindrops. When raindrops are very high in the sky, they start to freeze. The raindrops turn into hailstones. The hailstones get too big and heavy to stay in the air, so they fall to the ground.

centimetres wide fell in England.

The Ice Blanket

RIDEAU REGION, CANADA
JANUARY, 1998

It was so, so cold. Everything looked like glass. Even the trees looked shiny. People slipped on the streets and cars skidded on the roads. A thick blanket of ice covered everything!

What had happened?

Freezing raindrops had fallen. When lots of freezing raindrops start to fall, an ice storm begins. After most ice storms, the weather gets warmer and the ice melts. But this time, a second ice storm came, and then a third. The ice just got thicker and thicker. The ice on the trees was so thick that some branches cracked and fell off.

aeroplanes that fly through freezing rain.

Weird Weather Watch

Alpine mountains are usually covered in snow. One day in 2002, the mountains turned brown. They were covered in sand! Winds had picked up sand from the Sahara **Desert** 1,500 miles away!

In 2002, lightning hit a school in China. The lightning threw children out of their seats!

In parts of Spain, balls of ice fell from the sky in 2000. The ice balls were bigger than basketballs! Some of the balls were so big that they smashed through people's cars!

Rain usually has no colour, but in 2001, weird rain fell on a village in India. The rain was red, green and brown!

Glossary

desert   a very dry area of land

fog   a misty cloud of small water drops that collect close to the ground or over water

hailstones   balls of ice that fall from the sky during a storm

horizon   the line where the sea or flat land seems to meet the sky

hurricane   a large, powerful storm with strong winds and heavy rains

lightning   a flash of light in the sky caused by natural electricity in the air

mirage   a sight that seems to appear but is not actually there

reflect   to throw back light or sound from a surface

smog   a mixture of fog and smoke

volcano   an opening in the earth from which hot gases, lava and ashes are thrown up